The Muvipix.com Guide to
Adobe Premiere Rush

Steve Grisetti

Simplified moviemaking
for your desktop or
mobile devices

About Muvipix.com

Muvipix.com was created to offer support and community to amateur and semi-professional videomakers. Registration is free, and that gets you access to the world's friendliest, most helpful forum and lots of ad-free space for displaying your work. On the products page, you'll find dozens of free tips, tutorials, motion backgrounds, DVD templates, sound effects, royalty-free music and stock video clips. For a small annual subscription fee that we use to keep the site running, you'll have unlimited downloads from the ever-growing library of support materials and media.

We invite you to drop by and visit our thriving community. It costs absolutely nothing – and we'd love to have you join the neighborhood!

http://Muvipix.com

About the author

Steve Grisetti holds a master's degree in Telecommunications from Ohio University and spent several years working in the motion picture and television industry in Los Angeles. A veteran user of several video editing programs and systems, Steve is the co-founder of Muvipix.com, a help and support site for amateur and semi-professional videomakers. A professional graphic designer and video freelancer, he has taught classes in Photoshop, lectured on design and even created classes for lynda.com. He lives in suburban Milwaukee.

Other books by Steve Grisetti

Cool Tricks & Hot Tips for Adobe Premiere Elements
The Muvipix.com Guide to DVD Architect
The Muvipix.com Guides to Vegas Movie Studio HD 10 and 11
The Muvipix.com Guide to Vegas Movie Studio 14
The Muvipix.com Guides to Sony Movie Studio 12 and 13
The Muvipix.com Guides to CyberLink PowerDirector 12, 13, 14 and 15
The Muvipix.com Guides to Adobe Premiere Elements 7, 8, 9 ,10 ,11, 12 ,13, 14, 15, 2018, 2019 and 2020
The Muvipix.com Guides to Photoshop Elements & Premiere Elements 7, 8 , 9 ,10, 11, 12 ,13, 14 and 15
The Muvipix.com Guide to Photoshop Elements 2018, 2019 and 2020

An introduction

20 years ago (more or less) the camcorder world went digital. Gone were VHS camcorders and video digitizers. Camcorders were recording digital data to tape, and consumer camcorders and computers for the first time spoke the same language.

It changed everything, as far as video editing was concerned. On a basic home computer you could edit near-broadcast quality video. And while the professional world edited high-end digital video with programs like Final Cut and Premiere Pro, consumers were able to do similar things with affordable programs like Premiere Elements.

Consumer video continues to change, as do the systems we use to edit it. Fewer consumers shoot video on camcorders or DSLRs. More people are shooting video on tablets and phones. And you no longer need a desktop computer to edit it.

Premiere Rush was designed to live in this new world.

The program can be run on a desktop or a laptop computer – but its full-featured version also runs on phones and tablets. Its controls respond as effectively to a fingertip as a mouse click.

It is a simple and yet powerful app. And should you find yourself bumping into its limitations, you can open any of its works-in-progress in its professional big brother, Premiere Pro.

Rush is a great little programs with lots of obvious assets and more than a few hidden gems. And I'm excited to be able to share it with you.

I've no idea what videomaking and video editing will look like in another 20 years. But for now Premiere Rush serves quite effectively as a bridge between the old technology and the new.

Muvipix.com was created in 2006 as a community and a learning center for videomakers at a variety of experience and skill levels. Our community includes everyone from amateurs and hobbyists to semi-pros, professionals and even people with broadcast experience. You won't find more knowledgeable, helpful people anywhere else on the Web. I very much encourage you to drop by our forums and say hello. At the very least, you'll make some new friends. And it's rare that there's a question posted that isn't quickly and enthusiastically answered.

Our learning center consists of video tutorials, tips and, of course, books. We also offer a wealth of support in the form of custom-created DVD menus, motion background videos, licensed music and even stock footage. Much of it is absolutely free – and there's even more available for those who purchase one of our affordable site subscriptions.

Our goal has always been to help people get up to speed making great videos and once they're there, to provide them with the inspiration and means to get better and better at doing so.

Why? Because we know making movies is a heck of a lot of fun – and we want to share that fun with everyone!

Our books are a manifestation of that goal. And my hope for you is that this book helps *you* get up to speed. I think you'll find, once you get over the surprisingly small learning curve, making movies on your home computer is a lot easier and more fun than you ever imagined!

And you may even amaze *yourself* with the results.

Thanks for supporting Muvipix.com, and happy moviemaking!

Steve
http://Muvipix.com

The Muvipix.com Guide to Adobe Premiere Rush

Get to Know Premiere Rush

The Premiere Rush Interface

Basic Video Editing Moves

Chapter 1

Get to Know Premiere Rush

What's what and what it does

Easy to use and yet surprisingly powerful, Premiere Rush offers the simplicity of a basic video editor along with features to make even basic videos look great.

What is Premiere Rush?

In Premiere Rush, Adobe has combined the features of a simple, mobile device-based video editor with the more advanced features of a more professional editor.

Want to pull together a quick video and get it up on social media? You can do it in Premiere Rush. Want to dig a little deeper, to enhance the video and blend tracks of audio? You can do that too in Premiere Rush. Rush project files are even compatible with Premiere Pro CC so, if you find yourself banging against the limitations of Premiere Rush, you can finish your project in Premiere Pro, one of the world's most advanced video editors.

In fact, Rush is a part of Adobe's Creative Cloud app set, meaning not only can your projects be stored in the cloud for safekeeping and easy access, but many of the Creative Cloud's assets are available through the program, including a number of fonts, titles and templates.

Additionally, when the project files and media are stored in the cloud, the project can be edited from any device logged into your Creative Cloud account. In other words, you can begin editing your movie on your phone and finish editing on your desktop computer or laptop.

The interface

Premiere Rush uses a fairly simple interface, utilizing virtually the same interface on both desktop and your mobile devices. The workspace is clean and uncluttered, yet libraries of tools, adjustments and templates are available with just a click or two.

Dominating the interface are the **Monitor** and **Timeline**. Along the left side are tools for gathering and editing your media. Along the right side are tools for making adjustments to your timeline's media and for adding titles and transitions. Sharing or export options for your movies are accessed by clicking a tab in the upper left.

There are few preferences in the program, and the interface can't be modified or customized. However, by selecting the option under the program's **View** menu, the **Preview Quality** can be adjusted as needed to allow for the program's best performance on your device.

Basic editing moves

No matter what you plan to do with your video and no matter how creatively you plan to do it, the video editing process uses the same basic steps.

Here's a brief walkthrough of the steps you'll take for creating any video project in Rush.

1 Start a project

Starting a new project in Premiere Rush is as clicking the **Create a New Project** on the program's **Home** page.

Current projects are displayed under **Your Projects** on this **Home** page. As we discuss in **Chapter 2, Start a Project**, you can store your project in the Creative Cloud or on your computer or device.

You don't need to **Save** your Premiere Rush project before you close the program. The program automatically saves a copy to your device or the Creative Cloud as you work.

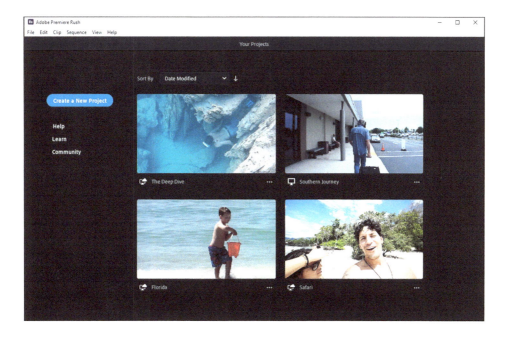

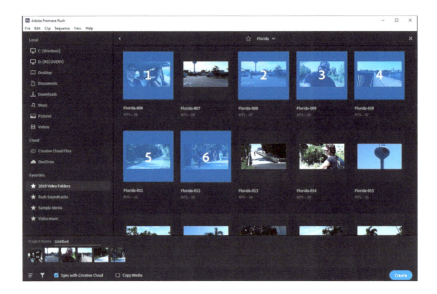

2 Gather your media

You can gather video, photos, music or other audio clips into your project by browsing to this media on your hard drive or by connecting to media in the Creative Cloud or other online storage, like iCloud or Microsoft OneDrive.

As you work, you'll likely name some locations as **Favorites** for easy access.

The media you import into your Premiere Rush project will be added directly to your timeline in the order you select it. Media you add to your timeline will also be added to your **Project Assets**.

We'll show you how to start a project in Premiere Rush and add media to your timeline in greater detail in **Chapter 2, Start a Project**.

3 Assemble and edit the clips on your timeline

Once you add your files to your timeline, you'll have a number of options:

- **Arrange your clips.** Once you've added media to your timeline, it can be easily rearranged by dragging and dropping clips to new positions. The clips on your timeline can also be deleted or moved to another video or audio track.

- **Trim your clips.** Trimming means removing footage from either the beginning or the end of a clip. To trim a clip, click to select the clip on your timeline and then drag in from either its beginning or end, as in the illustration on the following page.

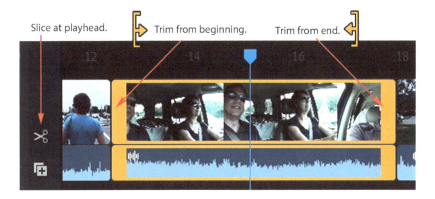

Slice at playhead. Trim from beginning. Trim from end.

- **Split your clips.** Splitting means slicing through your clips so that you can remove footage from the middle or delete a sliced-off segment completely. To split a clip, position the playhead over your clip and click the scissors icon to the left of the **Timeline**.

We'll show you how to edit media files on your timeline in **Chapter 3, Edit Your Timeline**.

4   Edit your audio

Music and other audio clips can be added and positioned on your timeline as needed and additional audio (voiceover) can be recorded directly to your movie.

If you have several tracks of audio, you can adjust your audio levels and mix your music and voiceover.

We show you how to add voiceover and mix audio in your movie in **Chapter 4, Edit Your Movie's Audio**.

5 Adjust your video

Once you've got your movie project assembled and edited, you can clean up and enhance it. The program includes professional-style tools for correcting and grading your video's color as well as for creating stylish video looks, for controlling playback speed, for creating collage or picture-in-picture effects and for adding transitions between your clips.

We show you how to use the complete video adjustment and effect tool set in **Chapter 5, Adjust Video Color and Effects**.

6 Add titles

Titles can be effective ways to explain scenes or to simply give credit where credit is due. Premiere Rush includes a library of title styles as well as links to an even larger library of styles and templates available through the Creative Cloud.

We'll show you how to add titles, download title styles from the Cloud and even how to create and save your own templates in **Chapter 6, Add Titles**.

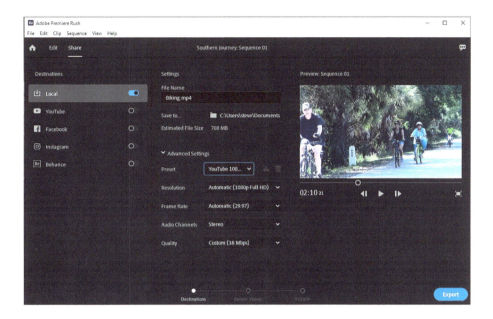

7 Share your movie

When you're happy with the movie you've created, you'll find a number of options for publishing it, as we discuss in **Chapter 7, Share Your Movie** We'll show you how to output your movie:

• **To your computer or device.** Rush can save your movie to your hard drive as an MP4 in a number of resolutions. The video can then be viewed on your computer, uploaded to a social media site like **Instagram** or used in another Premiere Rush project.

• **Online.** Using the tools built into Rush, you can send an optimized video directly from the program to sites like **YouTube, Facebook** and **Behance**.

And that's basically it!

You gather your assets, assemble them on your timeline, add effects, transitions and titles – then you share your masterpiece with the world.

But between these simple steps are the countless variations that can elevate your movie project from the realm of a basic structure to something truly amazing!

And that, of course, is what this book is all about.

Create a New Project

Gather Your Media

Manage Your Projects

Open a Rush Project in Premiere Pro

Chapter 2

Start a Premiere Rush Project

Assembling your assets

Premiere Rush is designed to get you editing as quickly and as easily as possible.

A few simple selections and you're reading to start building your movie.

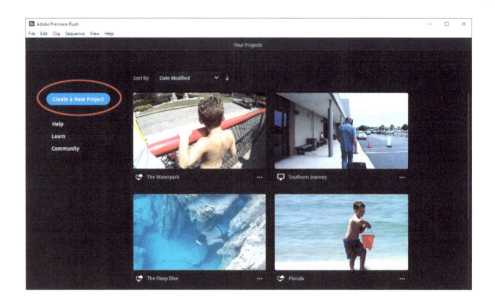

Start a new Premiere Rush project

Starting a new project is really as simple as clicking the **Start** button.

The program will base its project settings (aspect ratio, resolution, frame rate, etc.) on the specs of the video you add to your timeline. However, as we show you on page 14, you can customize your project's aspect ratio for your specific need.

1 **Launch a project**

New projects are launched (and works-in-progress are opened) from the program's **Home** screen – accessed by clicking the ⌂ icon in the upper left of the interface.

To begin a new project, click the **Create a New Project** button. (Alternatively, you can select the **New/Project** option under the program's **File** menu.)

2 **Name your project**

When you launch a new project, you'll be taken to the program's **Media Browser** screen, as illustrated on the facing page.

Although it's not necessary in order to proceed, it's a good idea to name your project by overwriting the word "Untitled" in the lower left of the **Media Browser**. This ensures you don't create several projects named "Untitled".

Existing projects can be renamed on the program's **Home** screen, as discussed on page 14.

Selecting the option to **Sync with Creative Cloud** will prompt the program to save your project file to the Cloud. Projects saved to the cloud will be accessible from any device logged in to your account.

Projects saved to the cloud can also be "un-synched" and saved locally to your device as discussed on page 14.

Browse to your media folder.

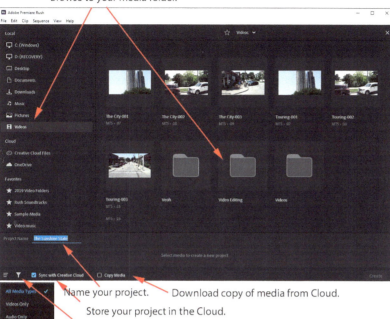

Name your project.   Download copy of media from Cloud.

Store your project in the Cloud.

Filter the media displayed.

3   **Locate your media**

The left side of the **Media Browser** displays your computer's or device's Libraries as well as any cloud storage your device may be linked to including your Creative Cloud Files, iCloud, OneDrive, Dropbox, etc.

Add frequently accessed directories to your Favorites

If there's a directory you frequently access while gathering media for your projects, you can name it a Favorite.

To designate a directory as a **Favorite**, browse to the directory. When the directory's name appears at the top of the **Media Browser**, click to activate the ★ next to the directory's name.

The directory will appear in the list of **Favorites** in the source listing along the left side of the **Media Browser**.

File directory folders can be accessed directly when added to Favorites.

When you select one of these sources, its folders and media will display in the **Media Browser**. Navigate to the video, still photos, music and other audio you'd like to include in your project. (Don't worry if all of your media isn't in the same directory folder.)

To save yourself having to always dig through several directories for a given media directory, your can name commonly-accessed directories as **Favorites**, as discussed in the sidebar on page 11.

The video and photos you select will appear in the order you've selected them in the lower left of the Media Browser.

4   **Select the media for your project**

Click to select the video, still photos and audio files you want to add to your project. As illustrated above, a number will appear over each media file as you select it indicating the order of your selection.

When your project is generated, your media files will be added to your timeline in the order you have selected them. (Although, of course, your media files can be re-arranged once your timeline is generated.)

You can add media from several directory folders by selecting as your browse. The video clips you select will appear in the order you have selected them in the lower left of the **Media Browser** screen, as illustrated.

If you are gathering media from an online or cloud source, it's a good idea to check the **Copy Media** option at the bottom of the interface, as illustrated at the bottom of page 11. **Copying Media** downloads a copy of any online media you select to your device, ensuring the media will be available to even when you are off-line.

When you've selected all or most of the media for your project, click the **Create** button in the lower right of the interface.

The program will prepare your media then switch to **Edit** mode. Your media will appear the program's **Timeline**.

5   **Add more media if necessary**

If you'd like to add additional video, still photos, music or audio to your movie, click the ⊕ button in the upper left of the interface· and select **Media**.

A small **Media Browser** will appear to the left of your timeline.

To return to the main directory for your computer or device in the **Media Browser**, click the **Back** arrow to the left of the current directory listing, as illustrated below.

To add more media to your timeline, click the ⊕ button in the upper left of the program.

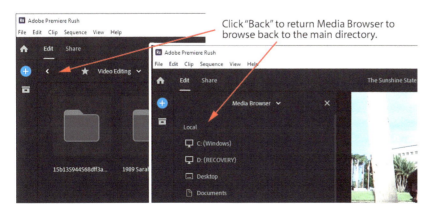

Click "Back" to return Media Browser to browse back to the main directory.

Change your project's aspect ratio

By default, your project's settings will be based on the specs of your source video. However, your project's **Aspect Ratio** can be manually set in order to, for instance, make your video more compatible to a social media site like Instagram.

To change your project's layout, click the **Aspect Ratio** button in the lower right of the **Monitor**. Options include **Landscape** (standard camcorder video), **Portrait** (upright phone video) and **Square**.

Newly selected media will be added to the end of your timeline. Music and audio only files will be added to the audio timeline, below the main video timeline, in the order it was selected.

The media you add to your timeline can be re-arranged, trimmed or sliced as discussed in **Chapter 3, Edit your Timeline**.

You don't need to **Save** your Premiere Rush project before you close it. The program automatically saves a copy to your device or the Creative Cloud as you work.

Managing existing projects

To open an existing project, click on the thumbnail the appears under **Your Projects** on the program's **Home** screen.

Change project name

To change an existing project's name, click the **...** button to the lower right of the project's thumbnail, as illustrated below, and select **Rename**.

Sync to or unsync from Cloud

To download a project from the Cloud and save it locally to your device, click the **...** button to the lower right of the project's thumbnail and select **Turn Sync Off**.

If you would like upload a locally saved project to the Creative Cloud, click the **...** button to the lower right of the project's thumbnail and select **Turn Sync On**.

Project saved on local device.   Project saved on Creative Cloud.

Project Save preferences

The location your downloaded media files are saved to is set in the program's **Preferences** (under the **Edit** menu on a Windows computer).

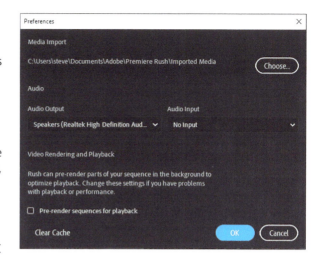

Supported media formats

Premiere Rush is capable of editing the following video formats: Apple ProRes, DNxHDm, DNxHR, Animated GIF, AVC H.264 (including M2T, M2TS and MTS), HEVC H.265 (with resolutions up to 8192x4320), M4V, MOV, MP4 and MXF as well as Sony XDCAM, SStP and XAVC 4K.

The following audio formats are supported: WAV, AIFF, MP3, M4A and AAC.

Open a Rush project in Premiere Pro

One of the nicest advantages to editing a project in Premiere Rush is that you aren't bound by the limitations of Premiere Rush.

If you find yourself bumping up against the limitations of Rush, you can open your Rush project in Premiere Pro, one of the most advanced moviemaking programs in the world.

If you select the option to **Open a Premiere Rush Project** from the Premiere Pro welcome screen, your Rush **Project** screen will open. Select your project by clicking on its thumbnail. Your project will open in Pro and a copy of the project will be saved as a Premiere Pro project. (The original Rush project will remain in your Rush library.)

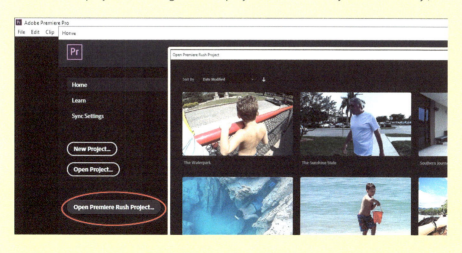

Arranging Your Clips

Trimming and Splitting

Adding Transitions

Working with Track Controls

Chapter 3

Edit Your Timeline

Building Your movie

Now that we've gathered our assets, we can actually begin the process of building our movie.

The Timeline is where our raw footage becomes a movie.

Assemble your movie

Building your movie is a combination of putting your video clips into an order that tells a story and getting rid of the stuff that doesn't.

The timeline in Premiere Rush is not nearly as powerful and versatile as the timeline of, say, a program like Premiere Pro or even Premiere Elements.

But, with up to four tracks of video and up to four tracks of audio available, you can do an awful lot!

Re-order your video clips

As you add media to your project, it is added to your timeline in the order it was selected. Video and photos are added to the main track on the timeline. Audio only files, including music, are added to an automatically-created audio track below the main video track.

New video and audio tracks can be added as needed. We'll show you how and why to add video audio tracks later in this chapter.

Re-arranging the order of your video and audio clips is as simple as dragging the clip or clips to new positions.

Timeline rippling

As you add media to your timeline, the main video track in Premiere Rush will "ripple". This means that, as video or audio clips are added or removed, the media to the right will move right (to accommodate the inserted media) or left (to fill the gap left by a removed media clip).

If you have several tracks of video or audio, these clips will also ripple as video is added or removed from the main video track. The audio or video clips on other tracks will also shift positions as you edit your main track.

Rippling means that, when a clip is added or removed from the timeline, the clips to the right move to allow for the insert or to fill in the gap.

Video and audio racks can also be locked so that the clips on these tracks hold their positions when the main video track ripples, as discussed on page 22.

If that sounds complicated, don't worry about too much about it. The ripple function in Premiere Rush is really very intuitive and you'll quickly get used to how it works.

Trim or split a clip

Trimming means removing video from the beginning or end of a clip on your timeline. To trim video or audio from the beginning or end of a clip on the timeline, hover your mouse over the end of the clip until the **Trim** tool (illustrated below) appears, then click and drag. The arrow on the **Trim** tool indicates which clip will be trimmed.

Splitting means slicing a clip on your timeline into segments. To split a clip, position the playhead at the point in the clip you'd like slice the clip and then click the **Scissors** button to the left of the timeline. (Alternatively, you can press the **S** key on your keyboard.)

If you have a clip selected on your timeline, the split will be made in that clip. If you have no clips selected, the split will be made through the video and audio on the main video track only.

Once a split has been made in a clip, you can delete or move one segment of the clip or you can insert a clip from **Project Assets** (see the sidebar on page 20) between the two segments.

Slice at playhead.   Trim from beginning.   Trim from end.

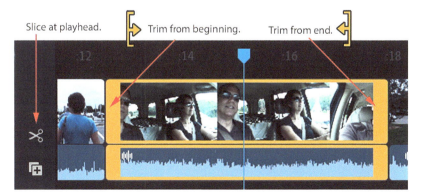

Project Assets

Any video or audio clip you add to your project will also be added to the usually unseen **Project Assets** panel.

Even if a clip added to your project has been deleted from your timeline, it will remain in your **Project Assets**, where it can be re-added to your timeline if the need arises.

To open the **Project Assets** panel, select **Project Assets** from the program's **View** menu.

The **Project Assets** panel will remain open on the left side of the program until you re-open the **View** menu and de-select it.

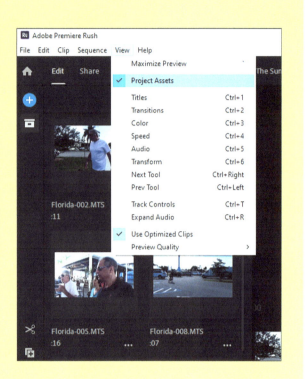

Duplicate a clip

If you'd like to reuse a clip (or a segment of the clip you've trimmed off) later in your movie, you can duplicate it.

To duplicate a clip, select the clip on your timeline and click the **Duplicate** button to the left of the timeline.

Add transitions

Premiere Rush comes with a small library of basic transitions. To access this library, click on the **Transitions** button on the right side of the program.

> **To apply a transition to the beginning and end of a clip** selected on your timeline, click on the transition in the **Transitions** panel.

> **To apply a transition between clips,** drag the transition from the **Transitions** panel to the intersection of clips on your timeline.

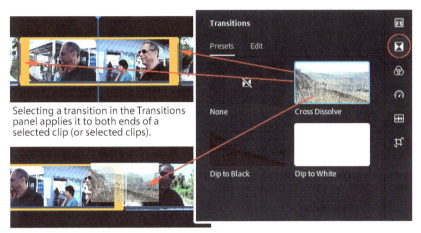

Selecting a transition in the Transitions panel applies it to both ends of a selected clip (or selected clips).

Dragging a transition onto the intersection of clips applies it between two clips.

The **Transitions** panel includes three pre-set transitions:

The **Cross Dissolve** transition dissolves from one video or audio clip to another.

Dip to Black fades to black between clips.

Dip to White fade to white between clips.

When added to the beginning of the first clip or the end of the last clip on your timeline, these transitions will create a **Fade In** or **Fade Out** for your movie.

Under the Transitions' Edit tab is a sider for adjusting the transition's length.

Set your transition's duration

To set the length of a transition on your timeline, click to select the transition and, on the **Transitions** panel, click the **Edit** tab.

A transition can be as short as 0.20 seconds or as long as 3.0 seconds.

Remove a transition

To remove a transition, click to select the transition between your clips and either press **Delete** on your keyboard or select the **None** option on the **Transitions** panel.

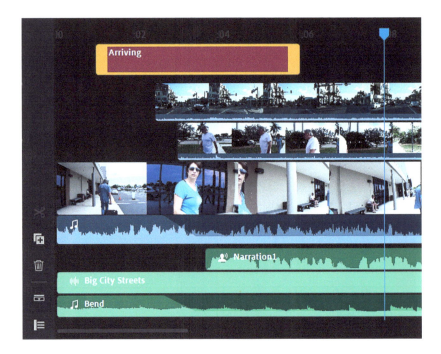

Multiple tracks of audio and video

In addition to the main video track, your Premiere Rush project can include up to three extra audio and up to three extra video tracks (which can include a video clip's accompanying audio).

Your audio tracks can include music, voiceover, sound effects or other ambient audio. Premiere Rush includes tools for mixing and blending several tracks of audio, as we discuss in **Chapter 4, Edit Your Movie's Audio**.

Your video tracks can include video or titles. Multiple tracks of video can be used to create **L-cuts** or **J-cuts** or to create **Picture-in-Picture** effects, as we discuss on pages 40 and 41 of **Chapter 5, Adjust Video Color and Effects**.

Add video and audio tracks

To create a media track, drag a video or audio clip or a title above or below the existing media on your timeline. (Video clips can be dragged to a new track from the main video track or from the **Project Assets** panel.) When you release your mouse button, the new track will appear.

Track Controls

Track Controls give you the ability to temporarily disable tracks of media as well as the ability to lock your clips' positions on the track. Audio track controls will also arm a track for recording, as we discuss in **Add Voiceover** in **Chapter 4, Edit Your Movie's Audio**.

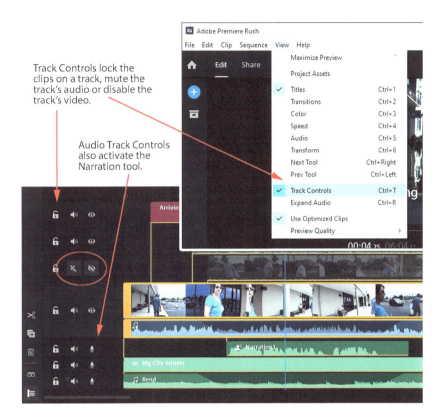

Track Controls lock the clips on a track, mute the track's audio or disable the track's video.

Audio Track Controls also activate the Narration tool.

Display Track Controls

To display the **Track Controls** on the **Timeline**, select **Track Controls** from the program's **View** menu.

Lock a track

Locking a track means locking the positions of all of the clips on that track so that they aren't affected by the main video track's **ripple** activity (as discussed on page 18).

To lock a track, click on the **Padlock** to the left of the video or audio track.

Disable a track

When a video track is disabled , the video on that track will be hidden or invisible. When an audio track is disabled , the audio on that track will be muted. Disabling certain tracks gives you the ability to focus on one or two audio or video sources rather than the entire movie's mix or composition.

To disable a track, click on the speaker (audio) or eyeball (video) on the **Track Controls**.

Audio can also be muted on tracks that include camcorder video clips in order to allow your music or voiceover to serve as your movie's audio.

Optimized playback and performance

The specs of the video you are editing as well as the effects you've added to it can affect the quality of your movie's preview as well as your system's performance. If you're seeing a reduction in preview quality or performance, there are a couple of settings worth getting to know.

In the program's **Preferences** (accessed under the **Edit** menu on a PC), you'll find

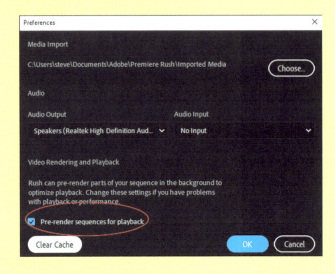

the option to **Pre-render sequences for playback**. When you select this option, the program will create temporary renders of your timeline so that your previews will look and play smoothly. Unless you find it negatively affecting your system's performance, I recommend checking it.

The **Monitor** in the program can be set to various **Preview Quality** levels.

If your device is struggling to play your timeline at full quality, you may want to set this quality level lower. Otherwise, you can find the option to set the **Preview Quality** to **High** under the program's **View** menu.

Finally, the program can cache rendered previews of your timeline to ensure the

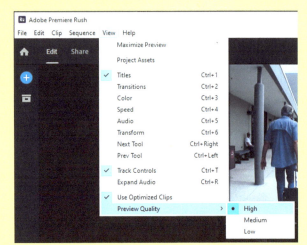

smoothest timeline playback with the least stress on your system's resources. You'll find the option to **Use Optimized Clips** under the **View** menu also.

If you find this cache become so full of previews that it's cutting into your device's storage space – or you just want to clean it out – you can clear it by clicking the **Clear Cache** button on the **Preferences** panel, as illustrated above.

Chapter 4

Edit Your Movie's Audio
Getting the sound right

Audio is at least as important a part of your movie as your video

And Premiere Rush has the tools necessary to clean up and mix your movie's soundtrack.

Your audio sources can include the audio included with your video, music, voiceover and even ambient sound or sound effects.

Premiere Rush includes a number of tools for getting the best sound quality from your audio clips as well as tools for mixing and blending several audio sources.

The Premiere Rush audio adjustments panel

The tools for adjusting, enhancing and mixing your audio sources in Premiere Rush are located under the **Audio** button on the right side of the program. The adjustments apply only the to clip you currently have selected on your timeline.

This panel includes both **Basic** and **Advanced** adjustments. These adjustments can be accessed by toggling the arrow to the left of each category's listing.

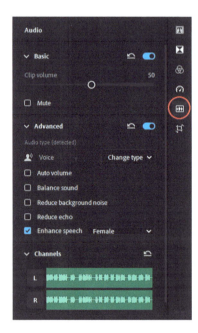

Basic and Advanced adjustments

Basic adjustments include a **Clip Volume** slider for controlling the selected clip's audio level and a **Mute** option for silencing the selected clip completely. All audio **Types** include the same **Basic** adjustments.

As we discuss on page 28, the **Advanced** adjustment options vary, depending on which **Type** of audio source clip you have selected on your timeline.

Any adjustment you make can be reset to its default by clicking the **Reset** button above that adjustment.

Reset adjustment

Channels

The **Audio** panel also displays a waveform representing the left and right audio **Channels** of your clip.

As you work with audio, you'll learn to recognize the ideal density for this waveform.

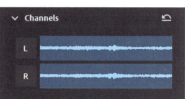

If your audio level is too high, it will sound overmodulated and distorted in your final movie output. As we discuss in the sidebar on page 28, the **Master Audio Meters** are the best indicators that your movie's audio is at an ideal level.

Auto Volume under the **Advanced** adjustments (see page 29) will automatically reduce or increase the clip's gain level and optimize your clip's audio levels.

Moving the **Clip Volume** slider under the **Basic Audio** adjustments will increase or decrease the volume of the clip on your timeline but will not affect the size of the waveform displayed under **Channels**.

Expand Audio view

By default, the audio tracks on the **Timeline** are minimized. The waveform representing the audio included with your camcorder video is minimized so much it is barely visible below the video thumbnail.

If you'd prefer to see greater detail in your audio clip, you can temporarily expand it by selecting an audio or video clip on your timeline and clicking the **Expand Audio** button to the left of the **Timeline**.

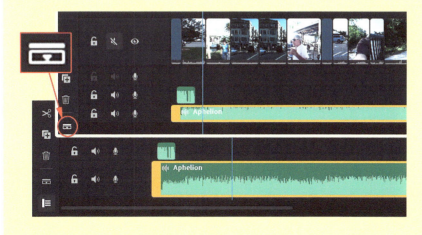

Master Audio Meters

In the lower right of the interface are little meters that indicate the audio levels for your movie as it plays. Pay attention to these meters! Don't trust the speakers in your computer or other device to represent your audio's level.

You'll ideally want your audio to register as full and green. An occasional yellow is acceptable, but if your audio is peaking in the red, you've got a problem.

Audio that is too loud ("overmodulated") can sound distorted and overloaded in your final movie. You may not notice it when you play your preview, but your final output will likely sound pretty bad.

Watch your audio levels! You may even want to isolate a track or clip by muting some audio (See **Track Controls** on page 22). Adjust your clips' **Advanced Audio** and **Basic Clip Volume** as necessary. And especially watch your **Voiceover** levels, which the program has a tendency to record rather hot.

You sure don't want your otherwise terrific video ruined by unintentionally grungy audio!

Voice vs. Music vs. Other audio types

Premiere Rush doesn't treat all audio clips equally. There are controls and adjustments available for some audio **Types** that aren't available for others.

Although Premiere Rush automatically assigns a **Type** classification to your audio clips, you can also manually set your audio clip **Type** by selecting it from the Audio adjustment panel's **Change Type** drop-down.

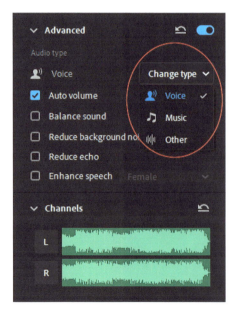

Voice clips have the largest number of audio settings. **Voice** settings include options for removing noise and for evening out the louder and quieter audio levels in your clip. We discuss these settings in greater detail on the facing page.

Music clips include an **Auto Duck** tool which automatically lowers the clip's level when there is a **Voice** clip on a parallel audio track. We show you how to use **Auto Duck** on page 32.

Other is the generic **Type** assigned to audio clips, including the audio that is included with your camcorder video.

Advanced Audio Adjustments

There are several adjustments available under the **Advanced** category on the Premiere Rush **Audio** panel.

Auto Volume (available for all types of audio) automatically raises or lowers your selected clip's gain so that the clip plays at a close to ideal volume level.

Balance Sound (available for **Voice** clips only) "compresses" your clip's audio levels (making quieter audio louder and louder audio quieter) to give your clip a more even audio level.

Reduce Background Noise (available for **Voice** clips only) uses a "noise gate" to silence the audio in your clip during pauses in your voiceover in order to reduce ambient and room noise.

The **Intensity** of this adjustment can be controlled using the slider that appears below it. Listen carefully to your results and try to work with the minimal level that fixes your issue. Too high of a setting can result in an overly-effected or unnatural sound.

Reduce Echo (available for **Voice** clips only), like **Reduce Background Noise**, uses an "noise gate" to reduce unintended room noise. And, like **Reduce Background Noise**, the **Intensity** of the adjustment can be manually set.

Enhance Speech (available for **Voice** clips only) includes enhancements for improving the overall sound of any recorded voiceover. It includes presets for **Female** and for **Male** voices.

Record a Voiceover

Voiceover or narration is a powerful storytelling device. In Premiere Rush, your **Voiceover** can be recorded directly to your movie's timeline.

1   **Arm a track for your voiceover**

Click the button on the upper left of the program and, from the option menu that opens, select **Voiceover**.

Alternatively, if the **Timeline's Track Controls** are open (see page 22), you can arm a track by clicking on a track's **Microphone** icon.

29

The armed track will display a red dot in place of the microphone icon.

If you get a message warning you that your selected audio device doesn't have an input, you will need to configure your audio settings in the program's **Preferences**.

Open the program's **Preferences** (under the **Edit** menu on a PC) and, on the **Preferences** page, select your microphone from the **Audio Input** drop-down menu.

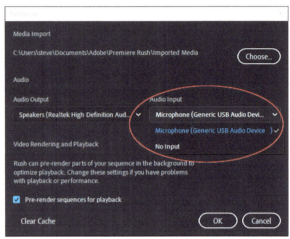

2 **Record your Voiceover**

Click on the red dot on the **Track Controls** to start the recorder.

The **Timeline's** playhead will back off a few seconds and a 3, 2, 1 countdown will be displayed in the **Monitor**. After the countdown, the program will begin recording.

Click the red dot again to stop recording.

Your voiceover will appear as a **Voice** audio clip on your timeline.

Pay attention to your audio levels as you record by watching the **Master Audio Meters** (see the sidebar on page 28). If you're recording too hot, your voiceover will sound awful and you'll likely not be able to salvage it.

Practice recording your voiceovers until you get a feel for what a good recording level feels like.

Audio mixing

Unless your movie includes only the audio from a single track of video, part of your editing process will include mixing several tracks of audio. This audio can include music, narration, ambient sound or sound effects and the sound that is included in your original camcorder video.

You can control you movie clips' audio levels and mix several audio sources three ways:

Clip audio controls

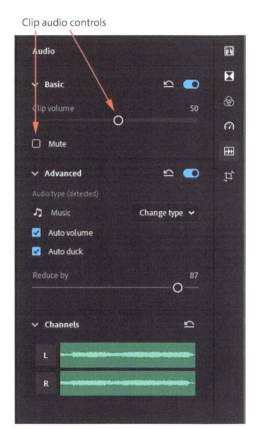

Raise or lower the audio level of a clip manually. As we discuss on page 26, when a clip is selected on your timeline, the **Basic Audio** adjustment panel allows you to raise or lower the overall volume of the clip.

You can't set a clip's audio levels to vary at specific points in Rush. Any setting is applied to the entire clip.

Mute a clip or track. Muting shuts off the audio completely for a clip or track of clips. You would mute a clip or track if, for instance, your timeline included a sequence of video clips and you'd like to hear your added background music rather than the video's original audio.

You can mute an individual clip by checking that option on the **Basic Audio** panel.

An entire video or audio track can be muted by disabling the track it on the **Track Controls**, as discussed on page 23.

Auto Duck your music. "Ducking" means lowering the audio level of your movie's background music whenever a narration or a voiceover clip is present on the timeline. As discussed on page 32, Premiere Rush's **Auto Duck** feature recognizes the presence of a **Voice** clip and automatically reduces the **Music** clip's level, then returns it to its normal level after the **Voice** clip ends.

Muted audio track

Auto Ducked clip

31

Auto Ducked music clip

Use Auto Duck to mix music and voice audio

The **Auto Duck** tool temporarily lowers the volume of a background **Music** clip whenever the playhead reaches a voice clip. (Before applying any adjustments, it is recommended that you ensure the audio levels of all of your movie's audio clips are optimized by testing them with the **Master Audio Meters**, as discussed in the sidebar on page 28.)

1   **Designate your Voice and Music clips**

    Auto Duck only affects the relationship between **Voice** and **Music** type clips. Ensure that your voiceover or narration clips are set up as **Voice** type clips and your music clip is set as a **Music** type.

2   **Select the Auto Duck option**

    With the **Music** clip selected on your timeline, check the **Auto Duck** option under the **Advanced Audio** adjustments.

An **Auto Duck** fade down will automatically be added to this **Music** clip whenever a **Voice** clip appears on a parallel track on your timeline. If you re-position your **Voice** clip(s), these **Auto Duck** fade downs will move to correspond to the new position(s).

3   **Adjust your Auto Duck level as necessary**

    The amount the audio level for your music is reduced during an **Audio Duck** can be controlled using the slider that appears under the **Auto Duck** option the **Audio** adjustments panel.

    By default, the music clip's audio is reduced to 87% during an **Auto Duck** fade down.

Color Adjustments and Grading

Size, Position and Rotation

Cropping and Vignetting

Creating a Picture-in-Picture Effect

Controlling Playback Speed

L-Cuts, J-Cuts and B Roll

Chapter 5

Adjust Video Color and Effects

Enhancing the look of your video

Sometimes reality just isn't good enough.

Premiere Rush includes a set of tools for cleaning up and even enhancing the look of your movie.

While Premiere Rush doesn't include a huge library of video effects, it does include a number of tools for correcting your video's color, for grading your movie's color for a more stylized look and for creating some cool special effects shots.

Color grading presets

Color grading is an art. It's what makes Hollywood movies look like Hollywood movies. Grading can set the mood for a scene or it give your movie an otherworldly look.

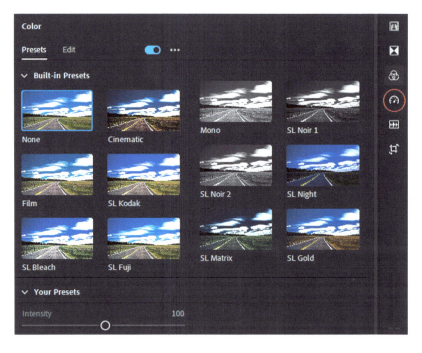

Premiere Rush includes nearly a dozen **Built-In Presets** for adding a mood, look or style to your movie. This library, illustrated at the bottom of the facing page, can be accessed by selecting a clip on your timeline and clicking the **Color** button on the right side of the program.

A **Preset** is e applied to a selected clip just by clicking on it. And you can return to the original look of your movie by selecting **None**.

Once you've applied a **Preset** to your clip, you can adjust its **Intensity** using the slider along the bottom of the panel.

You can also create and save your own **Preset** based on an adjusted version of a **Built-In Preset** or based on your personal **Color Edits** adjustment, as discussed in the sidebar on page 36.

Color adjustments

Under the **Edit** tab on the **Color** panel you'll find sliders for making your own personal color **adjustments** as well as for giving your video a stylish look.

Basic Color adjustments

Basic Color adjustments are designed to correct and enhance your clip's color and lighting.

The **Basic Color** adjustments are:

> **Exposure** corrects under-exposed and over-exposed video clips.
>
> **Contrast** increases or decreases the difference between the lightest and darkest areas of your video.
>
> **Highlights** enhances lighter areas of your video.
>
> **Shadows** decreases the difference between brightly lit and unlit areas of your video, salvaging details lost in shadows.
>
> **Temp** and **Tint** shift the color temperature or tint of a video to correct your clip's white balance or remove an unwanted color cast.
>
> **Vibrance** enriches and intensifies your video's color.
>
> **Saturation** increases or reduces the amount of color.

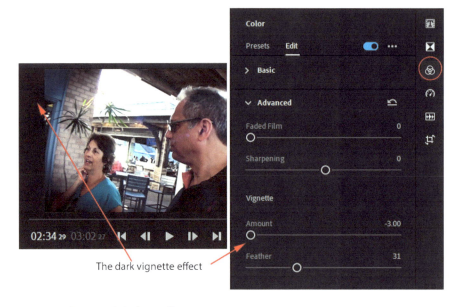

The dark vignette effect

Advanced Color adjustments

Advanced Color adjustments add special effects to your clip:

> **Faded Film** ages your video as if its color is fading.
>
> **Sharpening** increases the clarity of your video.
>
> **Vignette** adds a darker or lighter edge to your video clip. The **Feather** level controls how soft or sharp the vignetted edge is.

Save a custom preset

If you like the adjustments you've made to your video, you can save the look as your own custom **Preset**.

To create a preset based on your current **Color** settings, click the **...** (**More Options**) button on the upper right of the **Color** adjustments panel.

When prompted, name your **Preset** and click **Save**.

The presets you create will appear under **Your Presets**, below the **Built-In Presets** on the **Color Preset** panel.

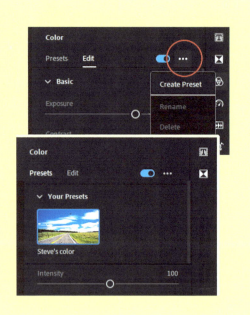

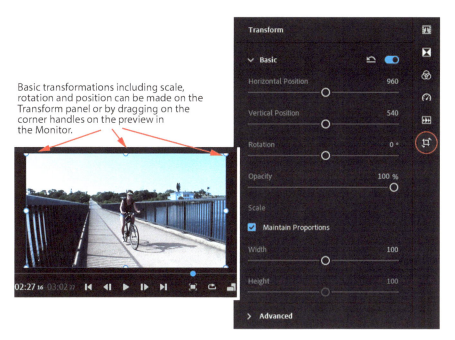

Basic transformations including scale, rotation and position can be made on the Transform panel or by dragging on the corner handles on the preview in the Monitor.

Transform your video

The **Transform** panel includes adjustments for changing the position and size of your selected video, rotating it, cropping it, making it semi-opaque and for adding a feathered edge to the clip.

These adjustments are accessed by clicking the **Transform** button on the right side of the program.

Transform adjustments can be undone by clicking the **Reset** button to the right of any transformation listing on the panel, as illustrated on page 38.

Basic transformations

The **Basic transformation** adjustments include sliders for changing your selected clip's horizontal or vertical position in the video frame, for rotating your video and for changing its size. However these changes can be made more intuitively simply the clicking on the video in the **Monitor**.

As illustrated above, when your video is selected in the **Monitor**, handles appear on its sides and corners. By dragging on these handles, you can enlarge or reduce the size of the video in the video frame.

If you hover just outside of these handles, a rotation indicator will appear. Click and drag to rotate your video.

Click and drag on the center of the video to change its position in the video frame.

These transformations can be used to create a **Picture-in-Picture** effects, as discussed on page 39.

Edge Feather applied

Advanced transformations

Advanced transformations can be used to change the shape and appearance of your selected video clip.

> **Crop** removes the sides, top or bottom of your video clip to focus on a detail in the video or to change the shape of the video within your video frame. (Note that **Crop** does not change the shape of your project's video frame itself. That is a function of the project's **Aspect Ratio**, as discussed in the sidebar on page 14.)
>
> **Opacity** affects the transparency of your selected video. 0% **Opacity** is complete transparency.
>
> **Edge Feather** adds a soft edge to your video. This soft edge is actually semi-transparent so, if you apply an **Edge Feather** to a video on an upper video track, the lower track of video below will be visible through the feathered edge.

Reset transformation

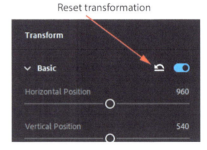

To remove **Basic** and **Advanced** **transformations** and return your clip to its default size, position and view, click the **Reset** button to the right of the **Basic** or **Advanced** listing on the **Transform** panel.

Create a Picture-in-Picture effect

Because Premiere Rush's **Timeline** can include up to three upper video tracks (in addition to its main video track), you can overlay your videos with smaller video clips.

Picture-in-Picture clip is on an upper track.   PiP is resized and positioned in Monitor.

To create a **Picture-in-Picture** effect:

1 **Add a video clip to an upper track**

   Drag a video clip from your main video track or from **Project Assets** (see page 20) to a video track above your main video. If there is no track visible above your main video track, drag your video clip to the **Timeline** right above the main video. When you release your mouse button, the new video track will be automatically created and your clip will drop onto it.

2 **Select and resize the video clip on the upper track**

   As noted in **Basic transformations** on page 37, you can adjust the size and position of a selected clip by using the sliders in the **Transform** panel or you can simply click on the video in the **Monitor** and adjust its size by dragging on the corner handles that appear.

3 **Position the Picture-in-Picture**

   Click on the resized clip in the **Monitor** and drag it to your desired spot in the video frame.

You'll likely want to mute the audio on the **Picture-in-Picture** clip so that it doesn't play along with your movie's main audio.

Control your video's playback speed

Using Rush's **Speed** adjustments, you can increase or reduce the playback speed of your video clip. This **Speed** adjustment needn't be applied to your entire clip, however. Rush's **Speed** adjustment can be applied only to a selected segment of the video.

The **Speed** adjustments for a selected clip are accessed by clicking the **Speed** button on the right side of the program.

1   **Set a Range for the speed effect**

The **Range** slider will by default show the speed effect applied to your entire video clip. Adjust the positions of the **In Point** and **Out Point** indicators so that only the portion of your clip you want to apply the effect to is selected.

2   **Set the Range Speed**

Your video can be slowed to 10% or increased to 1000%. As you adjust the clip's speed, the selected clip on your timeline will widen or narrow to indicate its changed duration.

3   **Select Speed options**

Your video clip can abruptly jump into its new playback speed or ease into it. Selecting the **Ramp** option will gradually shift your video into its new speed and then gradually shift it back again.

Selecting the option to **Maintain Audio Pitch** will keep your audio at approximately the same pitch so that as it slows down or speeds up with the video it won't pick up too much of a "monster" or "chipmunk" quality.

L-Cuts and J-Cuts

L-Cuts and **J-Cuts** are advanced storytelling tools, but they're easy to create and they're extremely effective ways to enhance your story with visual elements.

Suppose someone in your video is telling a story about their wedding day. It's a great story, but think how much more powerful it is if you include in your movie actual video or photos of the wedding or the incident he or she is describing!

An **L-cut** or a **J-cut** is merely a visual cutaway to this footage as the audio of the storyteller itself continues in the background.

Adding a cutaway is simple. Just drag the video or photos depicting the event (sometimes called "B roll") to an upper video track, over the main video on the **Timeline**. If there is no track visible above your main video track, drag your video clip to the **Timeline** right above the main video. When you release your mouse button, the new video track will be automatically created and your video clip will drop onto it.

Your movie will begin with the storyteller on screen then, as he or she speaks, it will cut to the B roll – often returning to video of the storyteller at the end of the story. (You see this technique used regularly on the evening news.)

An **L-cut** is a sequence that begins with the storyteller onscreen, then cuts away to the B roll. A **J-cut** is a sequence that begins with the B roll, then cuts back to the storyteller.

The terms "**L-cut**" and "**J-cut**" are artifacts from the days when film literally had to be cut into L or J shapes to create this type of effect.

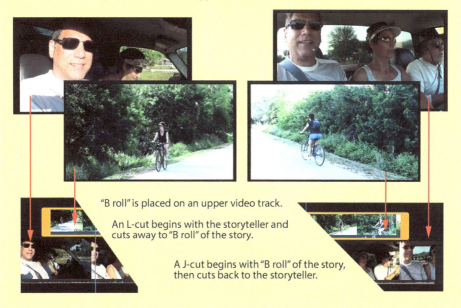

"B roll" is placed on an upper video track.

An L-cut begins with the storyteller and cuts away to "B roll" of the story.

A J-cut begins with "B roll" of the story, then cuts back to the storyteller.

Built-In and Cloud Libraries

Add a Title to Your Timeline

Customize Your Title's Text and Graphics

Add Transitions to Your Title

Chapter 6

Add Titles

Telling your story with text

Titles can help you tell your story by filling in the details.

They can also give credit where credit is due.

Premiere Rush comes with not one but two libraries of titles and text templates – a small library of templates or **Styles** built into the program and a much larger, ever-growing library available through the Creative Cloud.

The templates (or **Styles**) include stationary text, motion titles and titles for creating memes or calling out people or objects in your video.

Add a Basic Default Title

If you'd like to add a basic title to your movie, you can do so by clicking on the [icon] at the top left of the program and, from the menu the opens, selecting **Title**.

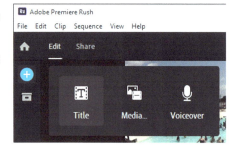

Your default title will be added at the position of the playhead on your timeline.

If there is no media on the main video track on your timeline, the title will be added to the main video track. If there is video on your timeline, a new video track will be created and your title will be added above the existing video.

When the title is added, it will appear in the **Monitor** with its default text selected. Type your text over this default text.

You can of course further customize your title by modifying its font, color, placement, etc., as we discuss in **Edit a title** on page 46.

To re-open a title on your timeline for customizing, **double-click** on it.

Built-in Styles library

Creative Cloud library

Add a Title template to your movie

Premiere Rush includes nearly 70 **Title** templates (**Your Styles**) in a variety of looks, from basic titles to lower thirds to call-outs to memes. (Lower thirds are titles that appear in the lower third of your video frame and are usually used to identify a person or location in the video. Call-outs are used to indicate or draw attention to a person or object in your video.)

The program can also access a much larger library of titles from Adobe's Creative Cloud (under the **More Titles** tab). Included among these are animated **Motion Titles**.

All of these templates are customizable and, once customized, your titles can be saved as your own personal templates, as discussed in the sidebar on page 49.

To access either of these libraries, click the **Titles** button the upper right of the program.

Add a Title Style

To add a title to your movie, drag it from the **Style** library to your timeline. If you add a template from the Creative Cloud, it may take a moment to download and install.

Once this template has been downloaded from the Cloud, it will appear under the **Your Styles** tab.

If you drag the title to the main video track on your timeline where video is already present, the video on your main timeline will ripple to allow you to insert the title (see **Timeline rippling** on page 18). If you add a title to an upper video track, the video on the main video track will appear as the title's background.

If there is not an empty video track on your timeline, drag the title to just above an existing video track. When you release your mouse button, the new video track will be created and your title will appear on it.

A template on the **Text** panel can be previewed by hovering your mouse over the **Style's** thumbnail. If are previewing a **Motion Title**, hovering your mouse over the thumbnail will preview the **Style's** animation.

Once you've added a title to your timeline, you can easily swap it for another **Style** by selecting the title on your timeline and then clicking on a different template under the **Your Styles** tab. (This does not work with templates that have not yet been downloaded from the Creative Cloud.)

Edit a title

Once a title has been added to your timeline, it can be edited and customized.

To edit a title, select the title on your timeline and, on the **Titles** panel, select the **Edit** tab.

Each text block and each graphic element includes its own set of customization options on the Titles Edit screen.

The title's customizations options for your title will vary, depending on the text and graphics included in the template. Each of these customizable elements will appear as a separate listing under the **Edit** tab, and you can access each element's setting by toggling its listing open.

Edit a title's text

To edit a text block:

1 **Select the text block**

With the title selected on the timeline, clip the **Edit** tab on the **Titles** panel. Toggle open the properties for text you want to edit. (A title template may include more than one block of text on it.)

The block of text will be highlighted in the **Monitor**. You can change or overwrite the text if you'd like.

2 **Change text properties**

With the block of text selected, you can change its font, style, size, line space (leading) and baseline shift.

You can also customize the selected text's color and add an outline or shadow to it. To change your font's color, click on the property's color swatch and select a new color from the **Color Picker** that opens.

Edit a template's graphics

When you toggle open the properties for a graphic element in your title, the graphic will be highlighted in your **Monitor**. By clicking on the swatches, you can change the color of the selected graphic and add or remove an outline or shadow, as illustrated on page 48.

More complex graphics may include additional properties including opacity, angle, distance and blur.

Reposition the title in your video frame

While you can't move around individual graphic elements in Premiere Rush **Title** templates, you can reposition the title so that, for instance, a call-out points to a person or object in your video.

To reposition a title, click on the title in the **Monitor** panel. When corner handles appear around it, drag title to a new position in the **Monitor**.

By dragging on these corner handles, you can also change the title's size and rotation, just as you can a video clip, as described in **Transform your video** on page 37.

Titles can be resized and repositioned within your video frame as needed.

Edit a Motion Title

A number of the **Styles** available from the Creative Cloud (under **More Titles**) are animated **Motion Titles**.

While you can customize the text, font and graphic elements in a **Motion Title** just as you can a standard title, you cannot customize or modify the **Motion Title's** animation.

Change a title's duration

By default, a title added to your timeline will appear as a 5-second clip. By dragging on either end of the title clip, you can increase or decrease the title's duration.

If you change the duration of a **Motion Title**, the animation will speed up or slow down to match this new duration.

Add transitions to your title

Transitions can be added to a title, adjusted or removed from a title just as they can be added to any video or audio clip (as discussed in **Add transitions** on page 21).

Premiere Rush's library of transitions can be accessed by clicking the **Transitions** button on the right side of the program.

When a title clip is selected on your timeline, selecting a transition in the **Transitions** panel will automatically apply that transition to the beginning and end of the title.

If you drag a transition onto the title clip, the transition will be added only to the end of the title you drag the transition to.

Save a custom Title Style

If you like the look or design of a title you have created on your timeline, you can save it as a custom **Preset**.

To save your title's design as a title template, click the **...** (**More Options**) button on the upper right of the **Titles** panel and select the **Save Template As** option.

When prompted, name your **Preset** and click **Save**.

Your new templates will be added to the **Your Styles** library.

Chapter 7

Share Your Movie

Outputting your final video

You've gathered your media. You've arranged your video to tell a story. Maybe you've added titles and music.

Now it's time to share the results with the world!

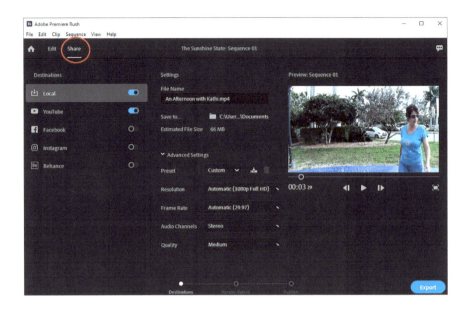

You're finished! It's finally time to share your little movie masterpiece with the world.

Premiere Rush offers a number of templates for outputting your movie and also includes tools for creating video for specific situations and even for uploading it directly to a couple of popular social media sites.

All of the output options are accessed by clicking the **Share** tab in the upper left of the program. You will need to slide the switch for each **Destination** to **On** in order to use that output option.

All of your movies will be output as MP4s.

Share your movie to your device

The most basic way to output your final movie is to output it to your **Local** device.

To share your movie to your device, ensure the **Local** option is switched on:

1   **Name your file**

Under **Settings**, type the **File Name** for your movie, overwriting the existing placeholder text.

2   **Select a save location for your movie**

Save To will list the default location your finished movie will be saved to. To change this location, click on the folder icon and browse to your preferred directory folder. **Estimated File Size** will display the approximate size of your output.

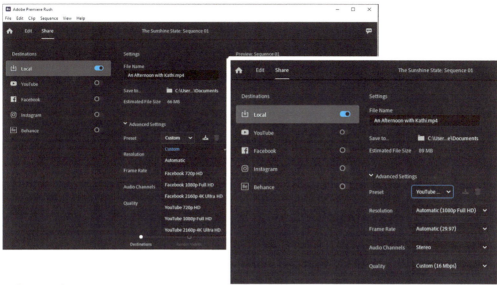

Advanced Settings

Toggle open **Advanced Settings** to set the resolution and other properties for your finished movie.

3   **Select a Preset**

The default **Automatic Preset** will be based on the properties of the source video on your timeline. The other **Presets** available under this menu will include settings for your output movie's **Resolution, Frame Rate, Audio** and **Quality**.

Presets

Based on a 16:9 (widescreen) project, the **Presets** available will include the following specs:

Facebook 720p HD: 1280x720 at a 12Mbps bitrate with stereo audio at your project's frame rate.

Facebook 1080p Full HD: 1920x1080 at a 12 Mbps bitrate with stereo audio at your project's frame rate.

Facebook 2160p 4K Ultra HD: 3840x2160 at a 24 Mbps bitrate with stereo audio at your project's frame rate.

YouTube 720p HD: 1280x720 at a 16 Mbps bitrate and stereo audio at your project's frame rate.

YouTube 1080p Full HD: 1920x1080 at a 16 Mbps bitrate and stereo audio at your project's frame rate.

YouTube 2160p 4K Ultra HD: 3840x2160 at a 40 Mbps bitrate and stereo audio at your project's frame rate.

Personally I don't believe you will see a huge difference between the **YouTube** and **Facebook Presets**, although the higher bitrate means the **YouTube** files will be larger. Not a lot larger, but larger.

Batch output to several destinations at once

Premiere Rush can simultaneously generate copies of your movie and upload them to several **Destinations** (**Local, YouTube, Facebook**, etc.) in one batch process.

To batch output your movie, prepare each **Destination** as described in this chapter and then switch on the **Destinations** you want to upload to.

When you click the **Export** button, optimized files will be generated for each **Destination** and, once you approve them, they'll be uploaded to each site.

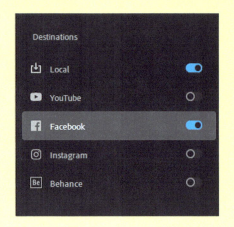

So, if you're going to upload these files to a social media site or view this video on a device, I would not be terribly concerned about the difference in quality between the two sets of presets. **Resolution** is the main property to focus on.

Aspect Ratios

The output **Presets** available under the drop-down menu will vary slightly, depending on the **Aspect Ratio** you've set for your project (See page 14).

> If your project's Aspect Ratio is set to Portrait (taller than wide), your available resolutions will be 720x1280, 1080x1920 and 2160x3840.

> If you've set your project's Aspect Ratio to Square, your available resolutions will be 720x720, 1080x1080 and 2160x2160.

Create Custom Settings

If you've prefer you can, of course, manually select your own properties for your finished movie. Your options for default widescreen are:

> **Resolution**: 1280x720, 1920x1080 and 3840x2160.

> **Frame Rate**: 23.967, 24, 25, 30, 50, 59.94 and 60 frames per second.

> **Quality**: Low, Medium and High bitrates. (Unless your file size is an issue, you should always select the highest quality for your files.)

Once you've customized your settings, you can save them as a **Custom Preset**.

Click the **Save Preset** button to the right of the **Preset** menu, as illustrated on the facing page. Name your **Preset** and click **OK**. This preset will then appear among your options under the **Preset** drop-down menu.

Output your movie

Once you've named and selected the properties for your movie, click the blue **Export** button in the lower right of the program. If the **Export** button in grayed out, make sure that the **Destination** button for your **Destination** is switched on, as illustrated above.

Before the program finalizes your video output, it will create a preview of your movie for you to review. If you're happy with the results, click the **Publish** button at the bottom center of the program and your video will be saved to your device or uploaded.

Before Premiere Rush saves your movie to your device or uploads it to a social media site, it creates a preview for your approval.

Authorize the connection to social media

In order to upload media directly from Premiere Rush to a social media site, you'll need to first authorize the link between the two. This is a one-time process. Once you're signed in, you're signed on your computer or device until you sign out.

But is a necessary first step before you can directly upload from the program to YouTube, Facebook or Behance.

To authorize this connection, click the **Sign In** button at the **Destination** and follow the prompts. Depending on how you've got your site's security set up, you may need to use your phone also to authorize this connection.

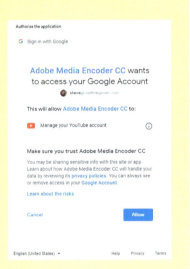

Upload your movie to a social media site

Premiere Rush includes tools for uploading directly to popular social media sites.

Share to YouTube

As discussed in the sidebar above, the first time you use the option to share to **YouTube**, you will need to log into your YouTube account from the program and authorize the connection. To do this, click on **the Sign** In button and follow the prompts.

Once you're signed in, the program will do the rest. To upload to YouTube, ensure that the **YouTube Destination** is switched on.

1   **Name your movie**

    As illustrated on page 57, the interface not only gives you options for naming your movie and creating a description but also for selecting the **Playlist**, setting the **Privacy** level and adding keyword **Tags**.

2   **Advanced Settings**

    By default, the program will create an MP4 based on your Rush project settings. If you'd like to customize those settings, toggle open the **Advanced Settings** and then select an existing **Preset** or create one of your own, as described on page 53.

3   **Select a Thumbnail**

    By default, the program will create a YouTube thumbnail for your movie based on the first frame of your movie. However, you can customize this thumbnail:

Advanced settings   Set custom thumbnail

To select a frame from your movie as your thumbnail, move the playhead in the preview to the frame you'd like use, then click the **Set Current Frame** button.

To add a custom frame based on a still photo on your computer or device, click the **Custom Thumbnail** button and browse to your photo.

4 **Export your movie**

Click **Export** to create your movie. If the **Export** button in grayed out, make sure that the **Destination** switch for **YouTube** is on, as shown at the top of page 52.

As illustrated on page 55, before the program uploads your movie to YouTube, it will create a preview of your movie for you to review. If you're happy with the results, click the **Publish** button at the bottom center of the program and your video will be uploaded.

Direct uploads to YouTube are usually limited to about 10 minutes. If you have an upgraded YouTube account that allows for longer movies, you may need to output any longer movies to your device (as described on page 52) and then manually upload them to YouTube through your web browser or YouTube app.

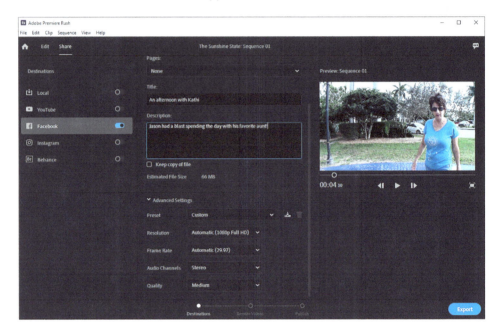

Share to Facebook

As discussed in the sidebar on page 56, the first time you use the option to share to **Facebook**, you will need to log into your Facebook account from the program and authorize the connection.

Additionally, Facebook does not allow you to upload directly to your personal account from a program. So before you connect to your Facebook account, you will need to go to Facebook and create a display page for your uploads.

To create a Facebook page, go to facebook.com/pages/create.

Once you've created a display page, click on the **Sign In** button and follow the prompts. Once you've signed into your Facebook account through the program, select the page you've created.

To upload to Facebook, ensure that the **Facebook Destination** is switched on, as illustrated above.

1   **Name your movie**

Name your movie and add a description of your movie under **Settings**. If you have more than one Facebook page, you can select which page your movie is uploaded to.

2   **Advanced Settings**

By default, the program will create an MP4 based on your Rush project settings. If you'd like to customize those settings, toggle open the **Advanced Settings** and then select an existing **Preset** or create one of your own, as described on page 53.

3   **Export your movie**

Click **Export** to create your movie. If the **Export** button in grayed out, make sure that the **Destination** switch for **Facebook** is on, as shown in the illustration on the facing page.

As illustrated on page 55, before the program uploads your movie to Facebook, it will create a preview of your movie for you to review. If you're happy with the results, click the **Publish** button at the bottom center of the program and your video will be uploaded.

If you want to upload your movie to your personal Facebook account rather than to your Facebook page, output an MP4 of your movie to your computer or device (as discussed on page 52) and then use your web browser or Facebook app to upload the file to your account.

Share to Instagram

Premiere Rush doesn't upload directly to **Instagram** from a computer.

To output your movie for Instagram, export your movie to your device using the tools under the **Instagram Destination** or save an MP4 using the **Local Destination** tools discussed on page 52.

When your movie has been output, use your web browser or Instagram app to upload the movie to your account.

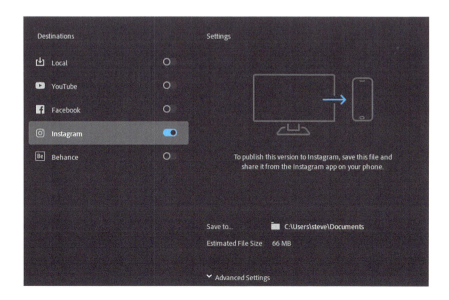

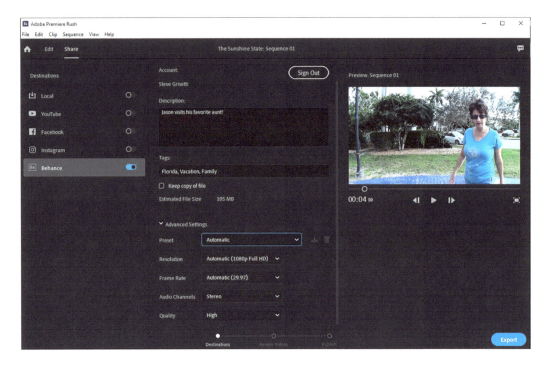

Share to Behance

As discussed in the sidebar on page 56, the first time you use the option to share to **Behance**, you will need to log into your Behance account from the program and authorize the connection. To do this, click on the **Sign In** button and follow the prompts.

To upload to Behance, ensure that the **Behance Destination** is switched on, as illustrated above.

1   **Add a description to your movie**

    Add a description of your movie and keyword **Tags** under **Settings**.

2   **Advanced Settings**

    By default, the program will create an MP4 based on your Rush project settings. If you'd like to customize those settings, toggle open the **Advanced Settings** and then select an existing **Preset** or create one of your own, as described on page 53.

3   **Output your movie**

    Click the blue **Export** button to create your movie. If the **Export** button in grayed out, make sure that the **Destination** switch for **Behance** is on, as illustrated.

As illustrated on page 55, before the program uploads your movie to Behance, it will create a preview of your movie for you to review. If you're happy with the results, click the **Publish** button at the bottom center of the program and your video will be uploaded.

Index

www.ingramcontent.com/pod-product-compliance
Lightning Source LLC
Chambersburg PA
CBHW041431050326
40690CB00002B/498